English

Assessment Papers

Stretch

8–9 years

Great Clarendon Street, Oxford, OX2 6DP, United Kingdom

Oxford University Press is a department of the University of Oxford. It furthers the University's objective of excellence in research, scholarship, and education by publishing worldwide. Oxford is a registered trade mark of Oxford University Press in the UK and in certain other countries

Text © Sarah Lindsay 2015
Illustrations © Oxford University Press 2015

The moral rights of the authors have been asserted

First published in 2015

All rights reserved. No part of this publication may be reproduced, stored in a retrieval system, or transmitted, in any form or by any means, without the prior permission in writing of Oxford University Press, or as expressly permitted by law, by licence or under terms agreed with the appropriate reprographics rights organization. Enquiries concerning reproduction outside the scope of the above should be sent to the Rights Department, Oxford University Press, at the address above.

You must not circulate this work in any other form and you must impose this same condition on any acquirer

British Library Cataloguing in Publication Data
Data available

978-0-19-274206-3

12

Paper used in the production of this book is a natural, recyclable product made from wood grown in sustainable forests. The manufacturing process conforms to the environmental regulations of the country of origin.

Printed in the UK by Ashford Colour Ltd

Acknowledgements

The publishers would like to thank the following for permissions to use copyright material:

Page make-up: OKS Group
Cover illustrations: Lo Cole

P12 'Facts: The Truth Behind the Loch Ness Monster' from www.channel.nationalgeographic.com/channel/the-truth-behind © 1996–2012 National Geographic Society. All rights reserved; p14 *The Midnight Fox* by Betsy Byars published by Faber and Faber Ltd; p25 'Weather' from *First Rhymes* by Lucy Coats, published by Orchard Books, 2004. Reproduced with permission from Hachette Children's Books; p30 'Talk to the Face' published in *First News* Issue 308, p10 (4–10 May 2012). Reproduced by kind permission of the National Deaf Children's Society; pp36–37 *Coraline* by Neil Gaiman, published by Bloomsbury Publishing Plc. (2003). Reproduced with permission.

Although we have made every effort to trace and contact all copyright holders before publication this has not been possible in all cases. If notified, the publisher will rectify any errors or omissions at the earliest opportunity.

Links to third party websites are provided by Oxford in good faith and for information only. Oxford disclaims any responsibility for the materials contained in any third party website referenced in this work.

Introduction

What is Bond?

The Bond *Stretch* titles are the most challenging of the Bond assessment papers, the number one series for the 11+, selective exams and general practice. Bond *Stretch* is carefully designed to challenge above and beyond the level provided in the regular Bond assessment range.

How does this book work?

The book contains two distinct sets of papers, along with full answers and a Progress Chart:

- Focus tests, accompanied by advice and directions, are focused on particular (and age-appropriate) English question types encountered in the 11+ and other exams, but devised at a higher level than the standard *Assessment Papers*. Each Focus test is designed to help raise a child's skills in the question type as well as offer plenty of practice for the necessary techniques.

- Mixed papers are full-length tests containing a full range of English question types. These are designed to provide rigorous practice, perhaps against the clock, for children working at a level higher than that required to pass the 11+ and other English tests.

Full answers are provided for both types of test in the middle of the book.

How much time should the tests take?

The tests are for practice and to reinforce learning, and you may wish to test exam techniques and working to a set time limit. Using the Mixed papers, we would recommend that your child spends 45 minutes answering the 75 questions in each paper, plus 5 minutes for reading the comprehension extract.

You can reduce the suggested time by 5 minutes to practise working at speed.

Using the Progress Chart

The Progress Chart can be used to track Focus test and Mixed paper results over time to monitor how well your child is doing and identify any repeated problems in tackling the different question types.

Focus test 1 — Spelling

> A letter string is a group of letters.

Match with a line, the words with the same letter strings but which make a different sound.

1. bruise — machine
2. catalogue — mallet
3. scheme — guide
4. wallet — tough
5. thought — drought
6. dough — tongue

> Watch out! Some of these word endings might change before the suffix is added.

Add the **suffix** *ous* to each of these words.

7. danger _____
8. outrage _____
9. mountain _____
10. vary _____
11. humour _____
12. fame _____

> Watch out! Not all words fit the rules.

Write the **plural** form of these words.

13. self _____
14. dwarf _____
15. elf _____
16. life _____
17. roof _____
18. half _____

Add *sion* or *tion* to each of these words to make a new word.

19 divide   _____
20 inform   _____
21 admire   _____
22 decide   _____
23 sense   _____
24 confuse   _____

Watch out! Again, some of these word endings might change.

Underline the **root word** in each of these words.

25 react
26 confession
27 dependant
28 moisture
29 premiership
30 punishment

Now go to the Progress Chart to record your score!   Total   30

Focus test 2 — Sentences

Add the missing commas to these sentences.

1. Jess was given a book new shoes and a watch for her birthday.
2. Mrs Pegg's class enjoyed art PE and English but not history.
3. In one day it poured with rain the sun came out and then it started to hail!
4. Oscar called Matt Luke and Tuhil to ask whether they wanted to meet at the park.

5–6. Water can enter a lake from streams rivers brooks and underground springs.

Rewrite the **proper nouns** with capital letters.

7–12. september   jacket   kite   nepal
       david   tuesday   grasshopper book
       york   chicken   wales   pencil

_____   _____   _____

_____   _____   _____

Complete the punctuation mark at the end of each sentence.

13. When are you going to pick me up____
14. You have to get on with your homework, now____
15. Jake's face dropped as his mum spoke to him____
16. You have read three of the books but don't forget the fourth____
17. I don't believe it____
18. Can you find the escaped sheep____

Add a different **conjunction** to each gap.

> A conjunction can also be called a connective.

19 The school fair was going really well _____ a donkey escaped!

20 Mrs Roberts helped Chloe with her spelling _____ she kept making careless mistakes.

21 The band kept playing loudly _____ they were asked to keep the noise down.

22 Laila went to buy some sweets _____ came home with a drink instead.

23 I found my mum's car keys _____ then we could drive home.

24 The car broke down _____ we had to push it home!

Write the following lines in a shortened form, using an apostrophe.

> For example, the hat worn by the gardener = the gardener's hat.

25 the dogs owned by the owners = _____

26 the microphone owned by the singer = _____

27 the sandwich eaten by Huw = _____

28 the glasses used by Laura = _____

29 the water drunk by the rabbits = _____

30 the kite flown by Meena = _____

Focus test 3 — Grammar

Clue: What does an adjective describe?

Underline the **adjectives** in these sentences.

1. The exhausted runner crawled to the finish line.
2. Jane loved her moth-eaten teddy.

3–4. The squelchy mud made its way into the holey boots.

5. The sun came out and gusty wind subsided.
6. Lucas gave up on his impossible homework.

Circle the **pronouns** in each sentence.

Clue: What does a pronoun replace?

7. The dog bit her hand.
8. Lola and Fred loved to visit their grandparents in Australia.
9. His book was ruined.
10. We must go quickly!
11. Jacob hurt my knee by accident.
12. Can she eat some of the cake?

Write six **adverbs** that could be used to describe the word 'ran'.

13–18 _____ _____ _____

_____ _____ _____

Write a more powerful **verb** for each of these verbs.

19. eat _____
20. sit _____
21. cry _____
22. walk _____
23. smile _____
24. go _____

Write a **comparative adjective** for each of these words.

> A *comparative adjective compares two things.*

25 large _____

26 slow _____

27 quick _____

28 sneaky _____

29 thin _____

30 hot _____

Focus test 4 — Vocabulary

Using a line, match each word with its correct definition.

1. picturesque — calm and peaceful
2. placid — a liquid for drinking
3. plaque — to prevent
4. potion — something that is preferred
5. preference — a beautiful scene
6. preclude — a plate fixed on a wall

Write a **compound word** using each of these words.

A compound word is a word made up of two other words.

7. to _____
8. back _____
9. day _____
10. eye _____
11. down _____
12. bed _____

Underline the **synonym** for the first word given.

Synonyms are words with similar meanings.

13	join	kick	link	apart	jumble
14	flood	attend	solve	spill	contain
15	linger	loiter	interrupt	interval	prevent
16	pester	despise	dislike	resent	hassle
17	blend	nasty	combine	indicate	mean
18	humorous	whole	thirsty	slurp	comical

Circle the **diminutives**.

19–24   piglet   cupboard   bucket   duckling

chicken   eaglet   lamp post   kitchenette

gosling   bullock   book   sheep

Put these words in **alphabetical order**.

gridlock   grandad   groovy

great   grand   griffin

25 _____

26 _____

27 _____

28 _____

29 _____

30 _____

Focus test 5 — Comprehension 1

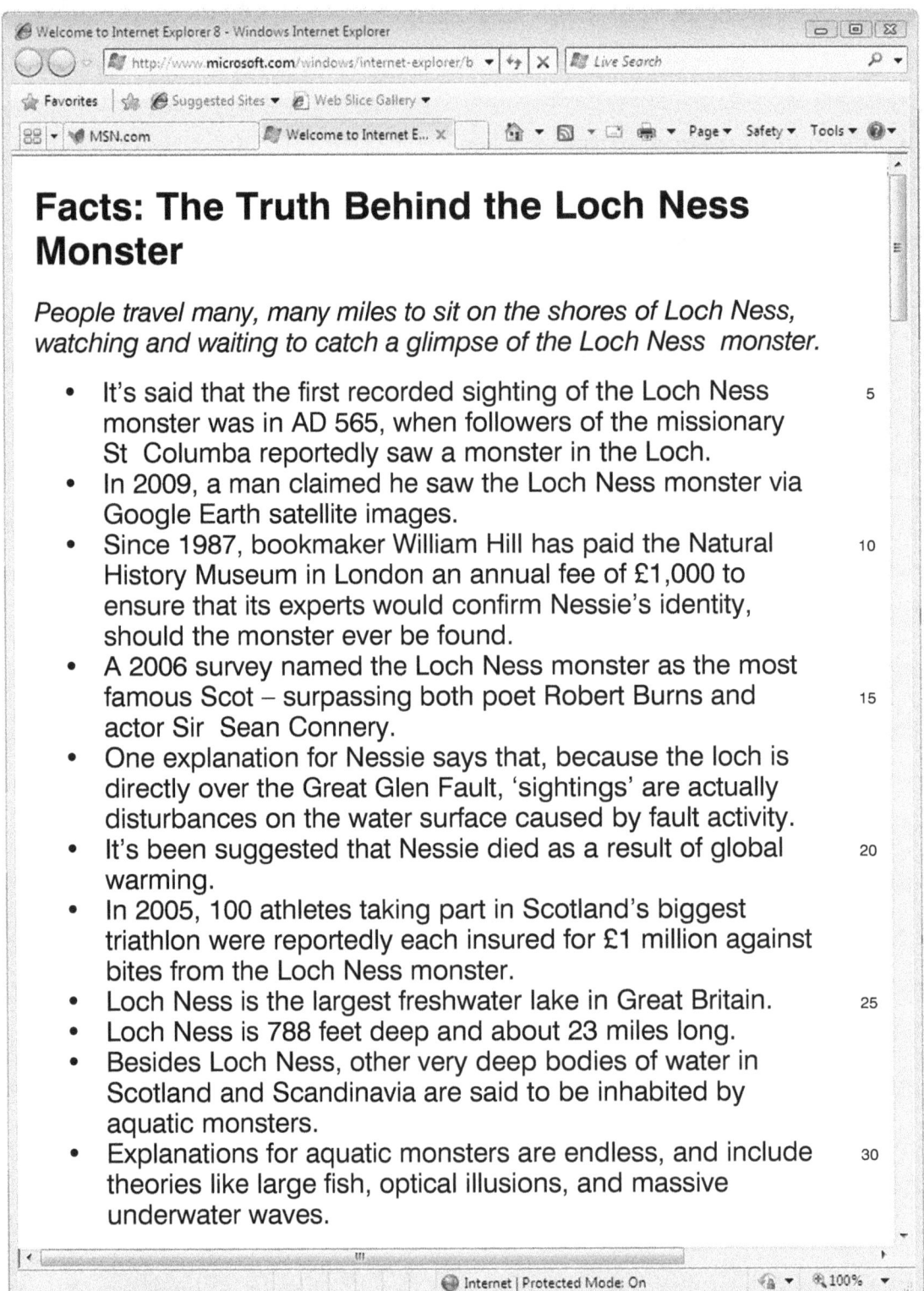

Facts: The Truth Behind the Loch Ness Monster

People travel many, many miles to sit on the shores of Loch Ness, watching and waiting to catch a glimpse of the Loch Ness monster.

- It's said that the first recorded sighting of the Loch Ness monster was in AD 565, when followers of the missionary St Columba reportedly saw a monster in the Loch.
- In 2009, a man claimed he saw the Loch Ness monster via Google Earth satellite images.
- Since 1987, bookmaker William Hill has paid the Natural History Museum in London an annual fee of £1,000 to ensure that its experts would confirm Nessie's identity, should the monster ever be found.
- A 2006 survey named the Loch Ness monster as the most famous Scot – surpassing both poet Robert Burns and actor Sir Sean Connery.
- One explanation for Nessie says that, because the loch is directly over the Great Glen Fault, 'sightings' are actually disturbances on the water surface caused by fault activity.
- It's been suggested that Nessie died as a result of global warming.
- In 2005, 100 athletes taking part in Scotland's biggest triathlon were reportedly each insured for £1 million against bites from the Loch Ness monster.
- Loch Ness is the largest freshwater lake in Great Britain.
- Loch Ness is 788 feet deep and about 23 miles long.
- Besides Loch Ness, other very deep bodies of water in Scotland and Scandinavia are said to be inhabited by aquatic monsters.
- Explanations for aquatic monsters are endless, and include theories like large fish, optical illusions, and massive underwater waves.

Answer the questions.

1 When is it said that the Loch Ness monster was first seen?

_____

2–3 In which country would you find the Loch Ness monster? Find two pieces of evidence from the passage to support your answer.

_____

_____

4–5 Why do you think the Loch Ness monster is so famous? Give two reasons.

_____

_____

6–9 What do some people believe the Loch Ness monster actually is? Give four theories.

_____

_____

_____

_____

10 Why were athletes insured for £1 million in 2005?

_____

11 William Hill, bookmaker, takes bets on whether the Loch Ness monster is real. Why is it important that an expert confirms Nessie's identity if it is ever caught?

_____

12–13 Describe Loch Ness in your own words.

_____

_____

14–15 'It's been suggested that Nessie died as a result of global warming.' (lines 20–21). What do you think? Give reasons for your answer.

_____

_____

Now go to the Progress Chart to record your score!   Total ( ) 15

Focus test 6 — Comprehension 2

The Midnight Fox

This is how Betsy Byars begins the story of The Midnight Fox.

Sometimes at night when the rain is beating against the windows of my room, I think about that summer on the farm. It has been five years, but when I close my eyes I am once again by the creek watching the black fox come leaping over the green, green grass. She is as light and free as the wind, exactly as she was the first time I saw her.

Or sometimes it is that last terrible night, and I am standing beneath the oak tree with the rain beating against me. The lightning flashes, the world is turned white for a moment, and I see everything as it was – the broken lock, the empty cage, the small tracks disappearing into the rain. Then it seems to me that I can hear as plainly as I heard it that August night, above the rain, beyond the years, the high, clear bark of the midnight fox.

To begin with, I did not want to go to the farm. I was perfectly happy at home. I remember I was sitting at the desk in my room and I had a brand new $1.98 Cessna 180 model. I was just taking off the cellophane when my mom came in. I was feeling good because I had the model, and all evening to work on it, and then my mom told me in an excited way that I was going to Aunt Millie's farm for two whole months. I felt terrible.

From *The Midnight Fox* by Betsy Byars

Answer the questions.

1 Where did the boy see the black fox leaping?

2–3 What image is the author describing when the fox is described as 'light and free as the wind'?

4–5 Describe the weather on the 'last terrible night'.

_____

_____

6 What is meant by 'the world is turned white for a moment'?

_____

_____

7 In the third paragraph what was the boy about to do when his mum came in?

_____

8–9 Why did the boy feel 'terrible' (line 19)?

_____

_____

_____

10 What triggers the memories of five years ago for the boy?

_____

_____

11 In which country do you think this story is based? Why?

_____

_____

12–13 Why do you think the empty cage is significant?

_____

_____

_____

14–15 What makes this an interesting way to start a story?

_____

_____

_____

Now go to the Progress Chart to record your score!   Total   15

Focus test 7 — Mixed test 1

Complete the table with **pronouns**.

> Pronouns are words that often replace nouns.

1–6

Pronouns about myself	Pronouns about others

Rewrite these sentences, adding the missing punctuation and capital letters.

7–10 barney the dog jumped up and down excitedly at the thought of a walk

_____

_____

11–15 where shall we meet you asked finn

_____

_____

Add the **prefix** or **suffix** *al* to each of these words.

> A prefix is a group of letters added to the beginning of a word, a suffix is a group of letters added to the end of a word.

16 option   _____

17 addition   _____

18 mighty   _____

19 season   _____

20 experiment   _____

21 together   _____

Circle the words that are neither masculine nor feminine.

22–26

prince	woman	aunt	twin
mother	nephew	duke	niece
child	teacher	woman	uncle
queen	cousin	fairy	father

Underline the **fronted adverbial** in each of these sentences.

> A *fronted adverbial* comes before the verb it is modifying.

27 Before lunch, I changed out of my P.E. kit.

28 Quickly and quietly, I hid behind the bush.

29 With blue flashing lights, the ambulance sped towards me.

30 Running fast, I tripped and fell on the pavement.

Focus test 8 — Mixed test 2

Add the missing double letters to each of these words.

1. pre ___ ___ ure
2. disa ___ ___ ear
3. po ___ ___ ible
4. gra ___ ___ ar
5. a ___ ___ ive
6. su ___ ___ ose

Circle the correct form of the helper **verb** in each sentence.

A helper verb supports the main verb.

7. A caterpillar is/were eaten by a bird.
8. Katie and Tim was/were going to Oscar's party.
9. Stan is/were hit over the head by Ned.
10. Tom is/were entering the speaking competition on Wednesday.
11. Sam was/were feeling sick during the night.
12. Caelab and Rufus was/were eating their sweets quickly.

Complete these word sums.

Watch out! The spelling of some words will need to change.

13. happy + er = _____
14. confess + ing = _____
15. red + er = _____
16. irritate + ed = _____
17. sense + ing = _____
18. thief + ing = _____

Underline the words that are spoken in these sentences.

19 "What is for lunch today?" asked Leah.

20 The children screamed, "Watch out!"

21 "Let's go for a walk," suggested Dad. "It will do us all good."

22 "You must be freezing in the cold wind!"

23 The dinner lady called, "It's time for lunch."

24 "Can we go waterskiing sometime?" asked Jess excitedly.

Add the missing **articles** *the*, *a* or *an* before these nouns.

25 ____ glass (specific)

26 ____ cloud (non-specific)

27 ____ light-bulb (non-specific)

28 ____ magazine (specific)

29 ____ igloo (non-specific)

30 ____ unicorn (specific)

> Articles are an example of a determiner. A determiner details whether a noun is known or unknown. 'The' is used if the noun is a specific thing or person. 'A' or 'an' is used if the noun is not a specific thing or person.

Now go to the Progress Chart to record your score!

Mixed paper 1

Queen Elizabeth I, the Queen of England from 1558 to 1603

Queen Elizabeth I was born on 7 September 1533. She was the daughter of King Henry VIII and Anne Boleyn. She grew up without a mother as in 1536, when Elizabeth was three years old, King Henry VIII ordered Anne's execution.

Elizabeth had an unsettled childhood with little interest from her father, though during this time she spent hour upon hour being educated by tutors. Due to this, she was one of the most highly educated monarchs of her time.

In 1554 Elizabeth was put into prison by her half sister, Queen Mary I. Just a few years later Mary died and in 1558 Elizabeth was crowned queen. She went on to rule the country for 45 years.

Elizabeth was a clever, well-educated woman who made shrewd decisions throughout her reign. This was vital for the stability of the country as she ruled during a time of unrest at home and rumblings abroad. Her reign has been named the 'Golden Age' when exploration, arts, literature, trade and music among other things, all thrived.

During Elizabeth I's reign, between 1577 and 1580, Sir Francis Drake was the first Englishman to sail around the world. Many items were brought back by sailors from foreign lands like potatoes and tobacco. Also a notable playwright during her time as queen was William Shakespeare. His plays are still watched and are popular, to this day.

Elizabeth always dressed well wearing beautiful clothes and many jewels. She felt she was the symbol of her country and wanted to portray it as a rich and independent empire.

She never married as if she had, her royal power might have passed to a foreign prince. She died in 1603.

Answer the questions.

1 Who was Queen Elizabeth's mother?

_____

2 What happened to Elizabeth's mother?

_____

3–4 Describe why you think Elizabeth had an unsettled childhood (line 6).

_____

_____

Focus test 1: Spelling

1. bruise – guide
2. catalogue – tongue
3. scheme – machine
4. wallet – mallet
5. thought – drought
6. dough – tough
7. dangerous
8. outrageous
9. mountainous
10. various
11. humorous
12. famous
13. selves
14. dwarves or dwarfs
15. elves
16. lives
17. roofs
18. halves
19. division
20. information
21. admiration
22. decision
23. sensation
24. confusion
25. act
26. confess
27. depend
28. moist
29. premier
30. punish

Focus test 2: Sentences

1. Jess was given a book, new shoes and a watch for her birthday.
2. Mrs Pegg's class enjoyed art, PE and English but not history.
3. In one day it poured with rain, the sun came out and then it started to hail!
4. Oscar called Matt, Luke and Tuhil to ask whether they wanted to meet at the park.
5–6. Water can enter a lake from streams, rivers, brooks and underground springs.
7–12. September, Nepal, David, Tuesday, York, Wales
13. When are you going to pick me up?
14. You have to get on with your homework, now! (A full stop is also correct but exclamation mark is a better answer.)
15. Jake's face dropped as his Mum spoke to him.
16. You have read three of the books but don't forget the fourth. (An exclamation mark is also correct.)
17. I don't believe it! (A full stop is also correct but an exclamation mark is a better answer.)
18. Can you find the escaped sheep?
19. *The school fair was going really well until a donkey escaped!*
20. *Mrs Roberts helped Chloe with her spelling as she kept making careless mistakes.*
21. *The band kept playing loudly although they were asked to keep the noise down.*
22. *Laila went to buy some sweets but came home with a drink instead.*
23. *I found my mum's car keys and then we could drive home.*
24. *The car broke down so we had to push it home!*
25. the owners' dog
26. the singer's microphone
27. Huw's sandwich
28. Laura's glasses
29. the rabbits' water
30. Meena's kite

Focus test 3: Grammar

1. The <u>exhausted</u> runner crawled to the finish line.
2. Jane loved her <u>moth-eaten</u> teddy.
3–4. The <u>squelchy</u> mud made its way into the <u>holey</u> boots.
5. The sun came out and <u>gusty</u> wind subsided.
6. Lucas gave up on his <u>impossible</u> homework.
7. her

ANSWERS

8 their
9 His
10 We
11 my
12 she
13–18 *quickly, slowly, speedily, carefully, quietly, coolly, comically, heroically*
19 *munch*
20 *slouch*
21 *sob*
22 *stroll*
23 *grin*
24 *leave*
25 larger
26 slower
27 quicker
28 sneakier
29 thinner
30 hotter

Focus test 4: Vocabulary

1 picturesque — a beautiful scene
2 placid — calm and peaceful
3 plaque — a plate fixed on a wall
4 potion — a liquid for drinking
5 preference — something that is preferred
6 preclude — to prevent
7 *today*
8 *backdoor*
9 *daytime*
10 *eyelid*
11 *downstairs*
12 *bedroom*
13 link
14 spill
15 loiter
16 hassle
17 combine
18 comical
19–24 *piglet, duckling, eaglet, kitchenette, gosling, bullock*
25 grand
26 grandad
27 great
28 gridlock
29 griffin
30 groovy

Focus test 5: Comprehension 1

1 The Loch Ness monster was believed to have been first seen in AD 565.
2–3 The Loch Ness monster is believed to live in Scotland. The passage mentions it as the 'most famous Scot' and then later refers to 'other very deep bodies of water in Scotland …' implying Loch Ness is one of them.
4–5 *The child's own thoughts on why the Loch Ness monster is so famous. They need to provide two reasons, for example the unknown element, the number of people who think they have seen it.*
6–9 It is believed that the Loch Ness monster could actually be:
disturbances on the water surface by fault activity
a large fish
an optical illusion
massive underwater waves.
10 Athletes were taking part in a triathlon race that meant they had to swim in Loch Ness. They were insured in case they were bitten by the Loch Ness monster!
11 It is important that an expert confirms the identity of the Loch Ness monster, in case someone tries to fake the body of the monster just to claim the winning money.
12–13 *The child's own description of Loch Ness including information on what it is, where it is, how long and deep it is.*
14–15 *The child's own response on whether they believe it is possible that the Loch Ness monster has died due to global warming. They need to give reasons for their answer.*

Focus test 6: Comprehension 2

1. The boy saw the black fox leaping over the grass by the creek.
2–3. 'light and free as the wind' implies that the fox is dancing around without a care in the world.
4–5. On the 'last terrible night' there was heavy rain and lightning.
6. 'the world is turned white for a moment' describes the moment a flash of lightning lights up the scene, enabling the boy to see it.
7. The boy was about to build a model in his bedroom.
8–9. The boy felt 'terrible' when he was told of the visit because he was happy at home and had no wish to leave his own comforts for two months.
10. The boy's memories are triggered at night with the rain beating against the windows of his room.
11. There are a number of clues in the passage suggesting that this story is set in the USA, for example the cost of the boy's model is in dollars and the fox is by a 'creek' rather than a stream. Also, the story refers to 'mom', an American expression for 'mum'.
12–13. *The child's own thoughts on why the empty cage is significant and why.*
14–15. The story begins with a look back at what happened first, then we get a suggestion about what happens at the end. Eventually the story begins. Usually stories have a beginning, middle and end.

Focus test 7: Mixed test 1

1–6. For example:

Pronouns about myself	Pronouns about others
I	They
Me	His
Mine	Yours

7–10. **B**arney, the dog, jumped up and down excitedly at the thought of a walk.
11–15. "**W**here shall we meet you?" asked **F**inn.
16. optional
17. additional
18. almighty
19. seasonal
20. experimental
21. altogether
22–26. twin, child, teacher, cousin, fairy
27. Before lunch
28. Quickly and quietly
29. With blue flashing lights
30. Running fast

Focus test 8: Mixed test 2

1. pressure
2. disappear
3. possible
4. grammar
5. arrive
6. suppose
7. A caterpillar is eaten by a bird.
8. Katie and Tim were going to Oscar's party.
9. Stan is hit over the head by Ned.
10. Tom is entering the speaking competition on Wednesday.
11. Sam was feeling sick during the night.
12. Caelab and Rufus were eating their sweets quickly.
13. happier
14. confessing
15. redder
16. irritated
17. sensing

ANSWERS

18 thieving
19 "What is for lunch today?" asked Leah.
20 The children screamed, "Watch out!"
21 "Let's go for a walk," suggested Dad. "It will do us all good."
22 "You must be freezing in the cold wind!"
23 The dinner lady called, "It's time for lunch."
24 "Can we go waterskiing sometime?" asked Jess excitedly.
25 the
26 a
27 a
28 the
29 an
30 the

Mixed paper 1

1 Anne Boleyn was Queen Elizabeth's mother.
2 Anne Boleyn was executed on the orders of Elizabeth's father (Henry VIII).
3–4 Elizabeth's childhood might have been unsettled as she didn't have her mother around and Elizabeth's father wasn't interested in spending time with her.
5–6 Elizabeth was put in prison by her sister in 1554 and then became queen in 1558.
7 Many things thrived during Elizabeth's reign, such as exploration, the arts, literature, trade and music.
8 'Shrewd' means showing sound judgement and common sense.
9 This line illustrates that life in England was unsettled with people feeling unhappy and challenging their circumstances. There were also similar feelings abroad.
10–11 Sir Francis Drake's achievement was particularly impressive because travel in those days was difficult with few seaworthy boats and little communication. There also was a lack of food supplies and health problems that would challenge an achievement like this.
12–13 Elizabeth felt that she needed to be a positive symbol for her country (line 24). She also felt unable to marry and let the country fall into foreign hands (line 26).
14–15 *The child's own answer suggesting two reasons why they believe Elizabeth's reign was worthy, for example she encouraged exploration, she reigned for 45 years in difficult times.*
16 irritable
17 accessible
18 objectionable
19 forcible
20 digestible
21 bled
22 blew
23 began
24 bent
25 broke
26 I've
27 we're
28 they'll
29 haven't
30 we'll
31–35 *The child's own sentences using listed nouns. Each sentence to have at least one underlined noun phrase.*
36–40 *sheep, fish, reindeer, fruit, jeans, pyjamas, scissors*
41 Yesterday Anil mistakenly picked up Josh's coat.
42 Laila went swimming then afterwards went to Jay's party.
43 Susie thought Lisa looked lovely in her new dress.
44 Brian easily slipped into his new boots before heading to the pond.
45 The Roberts were already waiting for the train when we arrived.
46 signature
47 capture
48 composure
49 departure
50 remeasure

51–55 *pretty*
dashed
chose
sensible
about

56–60 *handmade, handbag, handbook, handwriting, handout*

61 Tom shouted, "Shall we come too?"
62 "The swing is broken," said Niall sadly.
63 "Look out! There is a car coming," shouted Tyler.
64 Chloe asked, "When can we go on holiday?"
65 "Your homework has to be finished by tomorrow," said Mr Mead.
66 They'll have to hurry if they want to catch the train.
67 Do not forget to pick up Mum's coat too!
68–69 The children's dance was the best they'd seen in a long time.
70 The dog's (or dogs') bed needed a good clean because it was smelly!
71 Kelly walked cautiously in her high-heeled shoes, her skirt swishing around her legs as she did so.
72 Tikka, Korma and Pilau are the names of my chickens.
73 The boys raced to the park, jostling over who would get there first.
74–75 I ate many things for breakfast this morning, including toast, cereal and fruit.

Mixed paper 2

1 Each verse is about a different month in the year.
2 'Resolutions' in this context means 'New Year resolutions', a decision on something you intend to do for the year ahead.
3 In April the 'Earth wakes up', which suggests that plants will begin to grow; 'green things grow'. (In March the 'leaves peek out' is also correct.)
4 The line 'Lamb and foal' is used to illustrate the month that animals are often born.

5–6 Blackbirds sing in March. They are brave because it is still cold and windy during this month and therefore they are braving the weather.
7–8 The months June and July refer to the warmth of the days, for example 'Sun on skin' (line 18) and 'Heat and drought' (line 21).
9 The nights in November are cold as the temperatures drop and frost forms, therefore there is a crispiness about the ground.
10 In December the days are shorter and, therefore, there is more darkness about.
11–12 The first and third lines in each verse rhyme. Each verse is made up of three lines, starting with a month from the year.
13 Not all verses refer to the weather, for example May, August.
14–15 *The child is asked for their opinion of the poem. There is no correct answer though there needs to be evidence from the poem in support of their comments.*
16 examination
17 confusion
18 expansion
19 repetition
20 disruption
21 possession
22 occasionally
23 business
24 medicine
25 naughty
26 ei
27 eigh
28 ay
29 ey
30 eigh
31 The child watched as the carnival lorry went by.
32 As the bird sang the sun rose above the cloud.
33 The olive was picked from the tree.
34 The dog chased after the ball, causing chaos!

35 Which road do I take to get me to Oxford?
36 gym
37 pyramid
38 myth
39 Egypt
40 mystery
41 *Jake cried when Tom stood on his foot.*
42 *Leroy ran home but he arrived late.*
43 *A cyclist was knocked off his bike which damaged it.*
44 *Blood came from Katie's nose and covered her face and clothes.*
45 *As Meena slept the sun shone through her window, waking her up.*
46–50 *league, tongue, antique, unique, oblique*
51 to feel awkward or ashamed
52 pleasing, to agree
53 feeling or showing a happy, eager feeling
54 to feel very frightened, feeling terror
55 to feel full of shock
56–60 *duckling, piglet, owlet, minibus, eaglet*
61 No, I didn't know that.
62 What was that for?
63 Here I am, over here! (A full stop is also correct but an exclamation mark is a better answer.)
64 Where shall we go next?
65 My dog disappeared a week ago.
66 Let's go to the park <u>as</u> we might meet up with Terri.
67 I'm going to wear my boots <u>so</u> my feet don't get wet.
68 The book fell to the floor, <u>consequently</u> I lost my page.
69 I'm never going on that fair ride again <u>because</u> it is too expensive.
70 My dog barks <u>when</u> someone comes to the door.
71–75 "Look at that bird!" shouted Alice. "It is diving in the water to catch a fish."

Mixed paper 3

1 This article is written for hearing children.
2 National Deaf Children's Society
3–4 The NDCS are launching a campaign to increase awareness of how deaf children might feel and how hearing children can help in communicating with them.
5–6 The article suggests that deaf children can feel isolated, confused and not part of the 'group' due to being unable to follow what is going on.
7–8 Deaf children communicate through sign language, lip-reading or a combination of both.
9 The reporter has used Wembley Stadium as an example because it is a well-known place that most children know holds many, many people, therefore it gives a sense of perspective to the information.
10 A mainstream school can be attended by any child and doesn't specialise in providing education for any special group of children.
11–12 Firstly, all the chaos within the school can be distracting when a deaf person is trying to focus on a person speaking. Also, if a deaf person is able to hear a little, the background noise will detract from what is being said.
13–14 *The child's own answer, though it should make reference to the fact that if someone isn't looking at a deaf person when talking there is no way the deaf person can feel part of the conversation as the likelihood of them following what is being said is very small.*
15 *The child's own suggestion, for example wear ear muffs or try to communicate with friends without talking.*
16 fluorescent
17 science
18 fascinate
19 scenario
20 descent
21 reconsider
22 recondition or precondition
23 deactivate, reactivate

24 dethrone
25 rediscover
26 meddle
27 weather
28 knows
29 whine
30 prey
31 proper noun
32 collective noun
33 common noun
34 abstract noun
35 collective noun
36–40 *The child's own adjectival phrases using each of the given nouns. An adjectival phrase is a group of words that describe a noun, for example the whipping, gusting, ferocious wind.*
41 present
42 past
43 future
44 past
45 future
46–50 *chilly, cold, freezing, icy, nippy*
51 jungle
52 junior
53 juniper
54 junk
55 Jupiter
56 *great*
57 *peered*
58 *love*
59 *delicious*
60 *well-behaved*
61 I can't wait to go on holiday to Jamaica on a British Airways flight.
62 Tom's Midnight Garden is a great book.
63 Turn left into Delphia Avenue and then head straight on to York Station.
64 In 2012 the Olympics were held in London during July and August.
65 The French language can be tricky to learn.
66 Holly's puppies
67 London's underground
68 Ben's budgie
69 the children's coats
70 the residents' party
71–75 Dad arrived home just as we'd started tea. "Great to see you Dad!" they shouted.

Mixed paper 4

1 Coraline knew she was doing something wrong so was listening out in case her mother returned.
2 Previously the door had opened on to a wall of bricks.
3 The sound would have been satisfying to Coraline as she was achieving her aim of looking behind the door.
4–5 Coraline recognised the carpet and the wallpaper. This made her feel uneasy as she had just left her own home and now it seemed like she was walking in it again.
6 Although the picture was the same as that hanging in her own home, the boy in the picture had a different expression.
7–8 *The child's answer should include the fact that the woman in the kitchen was pale, tall, thin and fast moving.*
9 'her skin was as white as paper' (line 32)
10–12 *The child's own answer interpreting what Coraline might have found scary, for example going into a place that looked like her home, meeting people that looked like her parents, the fact that her 'new' parents had buttons for eyes.*
13–14 *The child's interpretation of what Coraline would feel like in the situation she found herself in, for example scared, confused, startled. Their answer needs to be supported with evidence from the passage.*
15 *The child should suggest that the boy's eyes may have been buttons.*
16 chiefs
17 cashier
18 perceive
19 beige

ANSWERS

20 retrieve
21 separate
22 particular
23 experience
24 popular
25 interest
26 finally
27 angrily
28 truly
29 dramatically
30 simply
31–36 Three sentences, each including two pronouns. A pronoun is a word that often replaces a noun, for example <u>He</u> caught a mouse, <u>it</u> was huge!
37 *because*
38 *hope*
39 *silently*
40 *brown*
41 *threw*

42–45

	Comparative adjective	Superlative adjective
great	greater	greatest
easy	easier	easiest

46 a word for someone or something
47 a word that describes someone or something
48 a 'doing' or 'being' word
49 a word that gives extra meaning to a verb
50 *odd*
51 *mean*
52 *fling*
53 *feel*
54 *stupid*
55–56 *Sentences illustrating 1. a groan (moan) and 2. grown (e.g. grown taller).*
57–58 *Sentences illustrating 1. rein (horse rein) and 2. a reign (a queen's reign).*
59–60 *Sentences illustrating 1. accept (when given something) and 2. except (with the exclusion of).*
61–75 The Jenkins family were on their way to Wales.
"Are we nearly there yet?" asked Tom.
"I'm so hungry."
"Not far," replied Dad.
Suddenly, there was a loud bang!
"What's that noise?" screamed Mum.

5–6 State two life-changing things that happened to Elizabeth in the 1550s.

_____

_____

7 Why was Elizabeth's reign described as the 'Golden Age'?

_____

_____

8 In the context of the passage, what does 'shrewd' (line 14) mean?

_____

9 What is meant by the line, 'unrest at home and rumblings abroad' lines 16–17?

_____

_____

10–11 What was so impressive about Sir Francis Drake's achievement?

_____

_____

_____

12–13 What responsibilities did Elizabeth feel as queen? Use evidence from the extract to support your answer.

_____

_____

_____

14–15 Do you think that Elizabeth I's reign was a worthy one? Give two reasons.

_____

_____

_____

_____

15

Add the **suffix** *ible* or *able* to make a new word.

16 irritate _____   **17** access _____

18 objection _____   **19** force _____

20 digest _____

Write these **verbs** in the past tense.

21 bleed _____   **22** blow _____

23 begin _____   **24** bend _____

25 break _____

Write the **contraction** for each of these.

26 I have _____

27 we are _____

28 they will _____

29 have not _____

30 we shall _____

Write five sentences. For each sentence, you must underline at least one **noun phrase**. You must include the listed **nouns**.

31 bucket

_____

32 swimming costume

_____

33 puddle

_____

34 statue

_____

35 flame

_____

Write five **nouns** that don't change in their **plural** form.

36–40 _____ _____ _____

_____ _____

Underline the **adverb** in these sentences.

41 Yesterday Anil mistakenly picked up Josh's coat.

42 Laila went swimming, then afterwards went to Jay's party.

43 Susie thought Lisa looked lovely in her new dress.

44 Brian easily slipped into his new boots before heading to the pond.

45 The Roberts were already waiting for the train when we arrived.

Add *sure* or *ture* to complete these words.

46 signa _____

47 cap _____

48 compo _____

49 depar _____

50 remea _____

Write a **synonym** for each of the underlined words.

51–55 The <u>cute</u> rabbit <u>ran</u> around its cage. Dan <u>decided</u> to let it out. It wasn't a <u>good</u> idea, now the rabbit was running <u>around</u> the garden!

_____

_____

_____

_____

_____

Write five **compound words** using the word 'hand'.

56–60 _____ _____ _____

_____ _____

Copy these sentences. Add the missing speech marks.

61 Tom shouted, Shall we come too?

62 The swing is broken, said Niall sadly.

63 Look out! There is a car coming, shouted Tyler.

64 Chloe asked, When can we go on holiday?

65 Your homework has to be finished by tomorrow, said Mr Mead.

Add the missing apostrophes in each sentence.

66 Theyll have to hurry if they want to catch the train.

67 Do not forget to pick up Mums coat too!

68–69 The childrens dance was the best theyd seen in a long time.

70 The dogs bed needed a good clean because it was smelly!

Add the missing commas to these sentences.

71 Kelly walked cautiously in her high-heeled shoes her skirt swishing around her legs as she did so.

72 Tikka Korma and Pilau are the names of my chickens.

73 The boys raced to the park jostling over who would get there first.

74–75 I ate many things for breakfast this morning including toast cereal and fruit.

Mixed paper 2

Weather

January new beginnings,
Resolutions,
Snow flakes spinning.

February frosty fogs,
Winter shivers, 5
Fire-warm logs.

March blows windy, smells of spring,
Leaves peek out,
Brave blackbirds sing.

April showers fall soft and slow, 10
Earth wakes up,
And green things grow.

May Day ribbons round a pole,
May-time babies
Lamb and foal. 15

June brings summer blazing in,
Scent of roses,
Sun on skin.

July joy means schools are out,
Time for picnics, 20
Heat and drought.

August goes on holiday,
Sandy castle,
Friends to stay.

September sees the autumn come 25
Plough the fields,
One by one.

October gales lash the trees,
Leaves a-swirling,
Crashing seas. 30

November nights all crisp and cold,
Winter coats,
For young and old.

December dark, yet full of light,
Christmas carols, 35
Stars so bright.

Lucy Coates

Answer the questions.

1 There are 12 verses in the poem 'Weather'. What do you notice about each verse?

2   In the context of this poem what does the word 'Resolutions' (line 2) mean?
   _____

3   In which line does it suggest plants are likely to start growing?
   _____

4   Why has the poet used the words 'Lamb and foal' (line 15)?
   _____

5–6 In which month do blackbirds sing and why are they referred to as 'brave'?
   _____
   _____

7–8 How many verses make reference to the warmth of the days? Use evidence from the poem to support your answer.
   _____
   _____

9   What is meant by line 13, 'November nights all crisp and cold'?
   _____
   _____

10 Why do you think December is described as 'dark'?
   _____

11–12 Describe the rhythm and patterns this poem uses.
   _____
   _____

13 Why is it slightly strange that this poem is called 'Weather'?
   _____

14–15 What do you think of this poem? Why? Use evidence from the poem to support your answer.
   _____
   _____
   _____

15

Add either *sion* or *tion* to make a word.

16 examina_____   17 confu_____
18 expan_____   19 repeti_____
20 disrup_____

Spell these words correctly.

21 posession _____   22 ocasionaly _____
23 buisness   _____   24 medisine   _____
25 nawghty   _____

Copy the letters that sound the same in each of these words.

26 vein   _____
27 weigh   _____
28 hay   _____
29 obey   _____
30 neighbour _____

Change these sentences, making all the plural **nouns** singular.

31 The children watched as the carnival lorries went by.
_____

32 As the birds sang, the sun rose above the clouds.
_____

33 The olives were picked from the trees.
_____

34 The dogs chased after the balls, causing chaos!
_____

35 Which roads do we take to get us to Oxford?
_____

Each of these words is missing a *y*. Rewrite the word correctly adding the missing letter.

36 gm _____
37 pramid _____
38 mth _____
39 Egpt _____
40 mstery _____

Rewrite these sentences and improve them.

41 Jake cried when Tom stood on Jake's foot.
_____

42 Leroy ran home but Leroy arrived late.
_____

43 A cyclist was knocked off his bike which damaged the cyclist's bike.
_____

44 Blood came from Katie's nose and covered Katie's face and clothes.
_____

45 As Meena slept the sun shone through Meena's window, waking Meena up.
_____

Write five words that end in *gue* or *que*.

46–50 _____ _____ _____
       _____ _____

Write a **definition** for each of these 'feeling' words.

51 embarrassed _____
52 agreeable _____
53 excited _____
54 terrified _____
55 aghast _____

Write five **diminutives**.

56–60 _____   _____   _____
_____   _____

Add the missing punctuation to the end of each sentence.

61 No, I didn't know that____
62 What was that for____
63 Here I am, over here____
64 Where shall we go next____
65 My dog disappeared a week ago____

Underline the **conjunction** in each sentence.

66 Let's go to the park as we might meet up with Terri.
67 I'm going to wear my boots so my feet don't get wet.
68 The book fell to the floor, consequently I lost my page.
69 I'm never going on that fair ride again because it is too expensive.
70 My dog barks when someone comes to the door.

Copy and punctuate these sentences.

71–75 Look at that bird shouted Alice It is diving in the water to catch a fish

_____

_____

Mixed paper 3

Talk to the face

Imagine missing out on talking with your friends while they are laughing and chatting all around you. That's what it can be like for deaf kids, but as Lucy Read from the National Deaf Children's Society explains, it doesn't have to be like that.

What did I miss?
Have you ever walked up to your friends when they're in the middle of a conversation and tried to work out what they're talking about? Or tried to follow a phone conversation just by hearing one side?

For deaf children lots of conversations can be like these – pretty hard to follow – but they don't have to be. The National Deaf Children's Society (NDCS) is supporting deaf young people to launch a campaign called Look, Smile, Chat, so that you can find out how to make chatting easy for everyone.

Being deaf
Someone who is 'deaf' might not be able to hear anything or they might be able to hear less than other people. If you think about how it might feel to be unable to hear very well, you can see why clear communication is really important.

Some deaf people communicate using sign language, while others read lips and speak, and some use a combination of signing and speaking. Whichever way people communicate, nobody likes to miss out on a joke or chat.

At school
There are 45,000 deaf children in the UK – that's enough to fill half of Wembley Stadium – and most go to mainstream schools like other children. There may well be one or two people at your school who have hearing loss.

Schools are noisy places, with lots of chatter, scraping chairs and people running around. This can make it even more difficult for deaf people to hear what's being said, which can make them feel left out.

A lot of people think that chatting with deaf people will be difficult because they won't understand you. But you don't need to worry – it's really easy once you know how.

NDCS has loads of tips to help you chat with deaf people your age.

When chatting with deaf children
- Turn to face them
- Talk normally, don't speak too slowly or shout
- Remember there are lots of ways to chat, including text or writing things down
- Check the person you're chatting with knows what you are talking about.

40

Answer the questions.

1 Who is this article written for?

2 What does the abbreviation NDCS stand for?

3–4 Why are NDCS launching a new campaign?

5–6 Describe what it might be like to be deaf.

7–8 How do deaf people communicate?

9 Why do you think the reporter has used Wembley Stadium as an example?

10 What are 'mainstream schools' (line 26)?

11–12 Look at the description of life in schools on lines 29 and 30. Why do you think these things make it harder for deaf people?

_____
_____
_____

13–14 Read again the tips to use when chatting to deaf children. Which of these do you think is the most important? Why?

_____
_____
_____

15 Suggest a way that one might be able to empathise with a deaf or partially hearing child.

_____
_____

Circle the words with a silent c.

16	magic	fluorescent	charity	clever
17	cleaner	complaint	coral	science
18	heroic	jockey	fascinate	childcare
19	scenario	neck	American	collapse
20	knock	backpack	descent	century

Add the **prefix** de, re or pre to each of these words to make a new word.

21 _____consider

22 _____condition   and   _____condition

23 _____activate   and   _____activate

24 _____throne

25 _____discover

Write a **homophone** for each of these words.

26 medal _____

27 whether _____

28 nose _____

29 wine _____

30 pray _____

Is each **noun** a **collective**, **abstract**, **proper** or **common noun**?

31 Buckingham Palace _____

32 swarm _____

33 high-wire _____

34 happiness _____

35 choir _____

Write an **adjectival phrase** about each of these **nouns**.

36 rain

_____

37 wind

_____

38 snow

_____

39 sun

_____

40 fog

_____

Write which **tense** each of these are written in, *past*, *present* or *future*.

41 is watching _____

42 was gliding _____

43 will run _____

44 has eaten _____

45 will write _____

Write five **antonyms** for the word 'hot'.

46–50 _____   _____   _____

_____   _____

Write these words in **alphabetical order**.

junk   junior   Jupiter   jungle   juniper

51 _____

52 _____

53 _____

54 _____

55 _____

Write a more interesting word for the words in bold.

56 It was **nice** to see Uncle James. _____

57 I **looked** through the keyhole. _____

58 We **like** to go swimming after school. _____

59 We ate a **nice** meal after the cinema. _____

60 My little sister was very **good** while her hair was cut. _____

Copy the sentences and add the missing capital letters.

61 i can't wait to go on holiday to jamaica on a british airways flight.

62 *tom's midnight garden* is a great book.

63 turn left into delphia avenue and then head straight on to york station.

64 in 2012 the olympics were held in london during july and august.

65 the french language can be tricky to learn.

Rewrite, adding the missing apostrophes.

66 Hollys puppies

67 Londons underground

68 Bens budgie

69 the childrens coats

70 the residents party

Copy and punctuate these sentences.

71–75 Dad arrived home just as wed started tea Great to see you Dad they shouted

Mixed paper 4

Coraline

Coraline and her family had moved into a new large house that had been divided into flats. Her parents were always busy and she often felt lonely and bored. One day Coraline thought she would do some investigating and she went to open the door at the back of their drawing room. It usually opened onto a wall of brick ...

The old black key felt colder than any of the others. She pushed it into the keyhole. It turned smoothly, with a satisfying clunk.

Coraline stopped and listened. She knew she was doing something wrong, and she was trying to listen for her mother coming back, but she heard nothing. Then Coraline put her hand on the doorknob and turned it; and, finally, she opened the door.

It opened on to a dark hallway. The bricks had gone, as if they'd never been there. There was a cold, musty smell coming through the open doorway: it smelled like something very old and very slow.

Coraline went through the door.

She wondered what the empty flat would be like – if that was where the corridor led.

Coraline walked down the corridor uneasily. There was something familiar about it.

The carpet beneath her feet was the same carpet they had in their flat. The wallpaper was the same wallpaper they had. The picture hanging in the hall was the same that they had hanging in their hallway at home.

She knew where she was: she was in her own home. She hadn't left.

She shook her head, confused.

She stared at the picture hanging on the wall: no, it wasn't exactly the same. The picture they had in their own hallway showed a boy in old-fashioned clothes staring at some bubbles. But now the expression on his face was different – he was looking at the bubbles as if he was planning to do something very nasty indeed to them. And there was something peculiar about his eyes.

Coraline stared at his eyes, trying to work out what exactly was different.

She almost had it when somebody said, "Coraline?"

It sounded like her mother: Coraline went into the kitchen, where the voice had come from. A woman stood in the kitchen with her back to Coraline. She looked a little like Coraline's mother. Only ...

Only her skin was white as paper.

Only she was taller and thinner.

Only her fingers were too long, and they never stopped moving, and her dark-red fingernails were curved and sharp.

"Coraline?" the woman said. "Is that you?"
And then she turned round. Her eyes were big black buttons.
"Lunchtime, Coraline," said the woman.
"Who are you?" asked Coraline.
"I'm your other mother," said the woman. "Go and tell your other father that lunch is ready." She opened the door of the oven. Suddenly Coraline realized how hungry she was. It smelled wonderful. Well, go on." 40

Coraline went down the hall, to where her father's study was. She opened the door. There was a man in there, sitting at the keyboard, with his back to her. 45

"Hello," said Coraline. "I – I mean, she said to say that lunch is ready."
The man turned around.
His eyes were buttons – big and black and shiny.

From *Coraline* by Neil Gaiman

Answer these questions.

1. Why was Coraline listening out for her mother returning?

2. What had previously been on the other side of the door?

3. Why do you think the author describes the turning of the key as a 'satisfying' clunk?

4–5. What did Coraline find familiar as she walked down the corridor? Why did this make her feel uneasy?

6. Something was different to Coraline's own home. What was it?

7–8. In your own words describe the woman in the kitchen.

9 Find an example of a simile between lines 30 and 35.

_____

10–12 List three things Coraline might have been scared by due to the situation she found herself in.

_____

_____

_____

13–14 How do you think Coraline felt at the end of this passage? Use evidence from the passage to support your answer.

_____

_____

_____

15 Having read the whole passage, what do you think the boy's eyes in the picture (line 25) might have looked like?

_____

Add *ie* or *ei* to each of these to make a word.

16 ch ____ ____ fs

17 cash ____ ____ r

18 perc ____ ____ ve

19 b ____ ____ ge

20 retr ____ ____ ve

Circle the word spelled correctly.

21 seperate   separate   seprate

22 particuler   particulr   particular

23 experience   experiance   expriance

24 popular   populer   populur

25 interst   intrest   interest

Make a new word by adding the **suffix** *ly* to each of these words.

26 final _____

27 angry _____

28 true _____

29 dramatic _____

30 simple _____

Write three sentences, each with two **pronouns** underlined.

31–32 _____

33–34 _____

35–36 _____

Write an example word for each of these word classes.

37 conjunction _____

38 abstract noun _____

39 adverb _____

40 adjective _____

41 verb _____

Complete the table.

42–45

	Comparative adjective	**Superlative adjective**
great		
easy		

Write a **definition** for each of these words.

46 noun _____

47 adjective _____

48 verb _____

49 adverb _____

Write a **synonym** for each of these words.

50 strange _____ **51** miserly _____

52 throw _____ **53** touch _____

54 foolish _____

Write each **homophone** into two sentences, illustrating their differences.

55–56 grown / groan

_____

_____

57–58 rein / reign

_____

_____

59–60 accept / except

_____

_____

Copy and correct this passage.

61–75 The Jenkins family were on their way to Wales

Are we nearly there yet asked Tom Im so hungry

Not far replied Dad

Suddenly there was a loud bang

Whats that noise screamed Mum

_____

_____

_____

_____

_____

Now go to the Progress Chart to record your score! Total 75